# The Stubborn Ear

Rosemary Lee Potter

WESTBOW*
P R E S S
A DIVISION OF THOMAS NELSON
& ZONDERVAN

Credits

The author credits family and spiritual friends, for assistance in developing this text, but with most gratitude to Christ's message about it, to which I listened. A special thanks to senior ministers, Dr. Thomas Farmer, Jr.; to Dr. Bert Blomquist, these now retired, Former Asst. Pastor, Rev. B.J. Foster, and Senior Pastor, Rev. Bob, Martin, our new pastors, for their messages of encouragement and educative reminders to listen to God, through all these years, even now, believing that He is always listening to us.

WestBow Press books may be ordered through booksellers or by contacting:

WestBow Press
A Division of Thomas Nelson & Zondervan
1663 Liberty Drive
Bloomington, IN 47403
www.westbowpress.com
1 (866) 928-1240

Set-up for first edition:
The text owes its publishing readiness to the creative skill of Dan Gerson (MySafetyHarbor.com); Staff of Sir Speedy Printing, Drew St., Clearwater, FL; Cover Design: Michael X Marecek; Author Photo: Michael Kelleher; and Life Touch Church Directory.

Author Contact:
Rose & Lee Press 585 Sky Harbor Drive Lot 133
Clearwater, FL 33759
727-712-8401 rosemary_potter@msn.com

ISBN: 978-1-4908-2835-0 (sc)

Library of Congress Control Number: 2014903873

Printed in the United States of America.

WestBow Press rev. date: 3/12/2014

# Dedication

This book of finding, hearing faith and direction is dedicated
to Robert and Kenyon, beloved sons, advisors, blessings.

It is also in remembrance of their father,
Robert Ellis Potter, who more than twenty years ago
became the real vision of listening to God.

— *RLP*

# Awareness Episodes

# THE STUBBORN EAR
### Rosemary Lee Potter

Be still and know that I am God.
— Psalm 46:10

Nobody would ever call me still. I am usually neither quiet nor still. My skill of mouth and mind, my energetic physical activities have been the basis of my various livelihoods—teaching school and swimming, writing, and, particularly, speaking. When I slept maybe I was still. All the while, I've certainly known that these verbal gifts were mine from God. That's what I've always told people. God apparently wanted glib me to rattle on and on. I thought, "Wasn't I being paid for my lively ideas both in print and speeches? Wasn't it God's gift that I am a faster listener than most of my friends speak to me?" Hmmm!

Twenty years ago I began to learn differently. It was then that my conscious Christian experience and human adventures gradually changed forever and I began to develop a quieter mouth, a better ear, and calmer mind.

My new walk began in 1992, when my husband Bob of twenty-eight years was diagnosed with melanoma. The ensuing family anxiety and eventual loss of my dear mate marshaled my attention to the meaning of Christian life. As events dramatically unfolded then and through the following years, I grew deeply conscious of God's daily presence, His constant concern, and His guidance in all the matters of living. I actually heard and saw answers to prayer. I became aware that I would receive guidance, if I would only finally shut up and listen. I'd learn how God wants me to occupy myself. I would never be the same.

This "stilling" memoir is a joyful sharing of what Christian life really is and what it can be for the Christian who gives over to constant praying and then, listens, paying close attention to God's messages and instructions. It's for those believers who may be, as I was, noisily too caught up in life's extremely unquiet busyness. It's a witness to believers, an urgent invitation to stop all this frenetic activity, to take notice that a Christian listens and does.

The read is also for those who do not yet believe. It is for those who are living each day frighteningly, confoundedly, open to dangerous temptations and drawn to and fro, convinced they are entirely on their own. This story confirms that God is real, His love, promises, concern, and instruction everlastingly ready, waiting only for our complete acceptance of Him and then attentive listening AND obedient following.

I've considered writing about this matter before, but something else always seemed to come up, a deadline, an invitation, something getting in the way of the work. During the last few weeks writing this book has become a deeply motivated idea. I've thought about it while sleeping, noted the ideas popping up in daily devotion books, on Christian radio, and even surfacing during Bible studies and sermons. It happened across me again and again.

When long ago I went to Billy Graham's Tampa Crusade at Raymond James Stadium with my sister, at our entry portal they gave us each an October. 1998 *Decisions* Magazine. I amused myself before the program started, while Libby went to get the pizza, by reading the last article. Written by Trica McCary Rhodes, a freelance author and California pastor's wife, it was entitled "Quiet Prayer, Abiding Rest." Rhodes' topic was strategies for making sure we take quiet time for our devotions, prayers, and thoughts. There it was again, this admonition about being still. She was quoting Psalm 46:10

A Tampa pastor read a poem he said someone had handed to him. Anonymous though the author was, the writer put forth the idea that God wants us to keep a "quieter mind." My own minister, Dr. Tom Farmer Jr., at St. Paul United Methodist church started his weekly newsletter with the words "Be Still," encouraging the church to have a totally silent listening hour once a week in the sanctuary, which seemed at first, for obvious reasons, a huge challenge to me. At a senior Bible Study he not only taught about angel messengers, he also described events in my own family that had spiritually moved him as my pastor.

Enough is enough! That did it! My stubborn ear has finally heard and will do! I'm burdened to write this book right now in peace and quiet, much in the same way I have shared aloud for twenty years the experiences and ideas, the awareness episodes related in it with family and friends, who kindly took time to listen. Perhaps the joy and surprise of my experiences will encourage others to be still and know, and do.

# Angel Visitors

This is the first time I have written about the God awareness-raising episodes that  happened during 1991 and 1992.

It had been a very long year, 1991, filled with hope and fear, alternately busying and exhausting. In February, my beloved husband of 27 years, Bob, had been diagnosed with deadly malignant melanoma. A surgery on the small black patch on the back of his left arm seemed successful. Wasn't he only off work for two days? Bob had asked that only our employers knew about the cancer and operation, not our grown sons, nor other family and friends. He wanted privacy in this matter and not a lot of attention paid to him about all this. I honored his wishes.

I remember wishing that we had others praying for Bob's healing. We certainly were in prayer ourselves. Maybe the doctor got it all. Yet, three melanoma cells were found in the associated glands that were removed. I was so naive as to think that with those glands and cells removed, the doctors got the cancer. It seemed to make sense.

We went back to work, Bob to the library position he so loved and the meticulous referencing of factual science and business information, I to middle school teaching. We were so confident about Bob's situation that we went on a big summer trip, still telling nobody about it. Along with sons Robert and Kenyon, we sailed on the Delta Queen, an authentic stern wheel paddleboat, steaming from

St. Louis out and back to St. Louis on the Mississippi River—off into the lakes of Kentucky and Tennessee. We loved it, all together again, flying kites at the stern, walking along the levees ashore, playing the calliope, and listening to ragtime piano music in the well-appointed old-timey salon.

It was as if Bob weren't ill at all. Once back at home, we followed all our routines, went to church, even bought a new car without buying credit life insurance. Talk about denial! Five days after we signed for the Caprice, Bob returned to the hospital, the melanoma resurfacing—a tumor erupting at the surgical site, now severe abdominal pains, now everybody in the family being told, praying, but filled with foreboding. I remember family members and friends being extremely unhappy with us that we had kept such a terrible secret. They made us promise never to do such a thing again. Soon most folks refocused on praying for Bob. He was put on the prayer list at church.

The treatment quickly moved from hospital oncology to the F. Lee Moffitt Cancer Center in Tampa. Now Bob would undergo aggressive treatment—high-dose chemotherapy and a bone marrow transplant—daunting procedures with high risks of their own. First, Bob's own marrow would be harvested and cryogenically stored for later return replacement. Then high-dose chemicals, some of which were so new, that, as his wife, I had to give special permission to try them, were dripped into Bob's veins, hoping to kill the deadly disease, while not killing him.

There would be a low point, I was warned, when Bob would have no natural defenses with which to fight off infection, when he would need oxygen assistance. Then he would hopefully begin to recover and receive his bone marrow back, hopefully "cleansed. "— cancer free. No guarantee, though. We kept on praying for healing, particularly for healing soon. Everything seemed to take so long.

At times I thought how strange it was that Bob seemed and looked so strong, limbs sound, his legs so muscular from all his years of walking and hiking great distances even around Clearwater. I'd look at him there in bed and be glad he was young, only 52. I thought, again naively, his body surely could and would beat this awful skin cancer.

Now that Bob's "fighting" marrow was gone, stored in two deep cold facilities, awaiting his later need, any infection could be deadly. His new room was kept free of air-borne infections with a special stream of air. When we visited him one at a time, we had to wash our hands well outside the room with antiseptic cleanser, put on a cotton gown from the laundry stack, and a surgical mask before entering. We couldn't take anything into the room. Even paper goods had to be sanitized in some kind of autoclave machine. We read Bob's cards to him from a distance. We couldn't even touch him. How I longed to hold him and kiss him.

One night at home, in the days just before the transplant, when I was once again praying for God's help in healing, if healing Bob was His will, a Bible story suddenly came to mind. I remembered the woman in the Gospel of Matthew 9:20-22, the one who had an issue of blood for more than twelve years! Yet, she had such faith in Jesus' healing power that she reached out and touched the hem of his garment as He passed by in the crowd. Jesus knew she'd touched the garment and turned to her. Due to her faith in His ability to heal her, He instantly did so, did what no other doctor had been able to do in a dozen years! As I thought of this Biblical faith-healing instance, I did not envision Jesus passing by me. Yet, from where I knelt, I still reached out across my own bed, reaching for that hem, imploring God to help Bob, if it were His will to do so.

Over at Moffitt, Bob had begun the treatment process, first the harvesting of his bone marrow from his hip. Then came the chemo. The experience exhausted Bob and deepened my fear. The silence of the treatment added to our unrelenting worry, although Bob wasn't in much discomfort. The chemicals dripped into his arm ever so silently, silent warriors against a silent, invading foe!

Next there would be that low point as the chemicals began to have their way hopefully in a successful fight against the ever invading melanoma cells, Soon Bob would reach that point in the battle where his body had literally no defense to fight infection or trauma. We never could have imagined that something even worse could happen at that very moment, yet it did.

At dawn I received a call that Bob needed immediate abdominal surgery—without which, he would surely die! I recall it was something in the cancer's vicious spread to his abdomen. Even if he survived the surgery, they said, he was in grave danger of dying from peritonitis from the infectious stomach fluids involved. Permissions were given, Bob, now in agony to the extent that he couldn't stand anyone to touch him, told me good-bye, "to remember him and his blue eyes."

He said. "I'll see you here or I'll see you in heaven," and was rushed away into a waiting elevator.

Dr. Thomas E. Farmer, Jr., our pastor, arrived and sat with my son Robert and me in the mezzanine waiting area near the surgical door. Dr. Tom walked over to a phone and activated our prayer wheel at church. When prayer wheel members, about eighty persons, are contacted, they drop everything and kneel, praying to God for His healing, the surgery to be a success. And so they were doing for Bob.

We'd been told the operation would take about three hours. The three hours passed without a word from Moffitt nurses or staff. During that vigil, and, even before Dr. Tom joined us, I was drawn, as I am today, to the Bible, the Psalms, in particular Psalm 116, which I read over and over in the little New Testament Bob had given me almost twenty-seven years earlier—right before our wedding.

I was particularly drawn to verses 8 and 9:
For you have delivered my soul from death,
my eyes from tears, and my feet from falling.
I will walk before the Lord in the land of the living.

The divided doors to the surgical unit suddenly swung open and the surgeon emerged and slowly approached us. It had been nearly five hours since Bob went into surgery. Dr. Tom took my hand in his. He would later tell me that, from his experience, when he saw the doctor, he thought the worst, owing to how exhausted and strained the doctor appeared. The man slumped into a chair opposite us and leaned forward.

Strangely, the doctor was shaking his head while he told us good and unusual news. We learned that Bob, who had entered surgery with no physical reserve to fight trauma or infection, had endured everything and was, in fact, awake, back in his room recovering! Praise God!

It seemed the doctor, now totally drained of energy, had finished two operations just prior to Bob's and had operated on him because it was a dire emergency! He quietly made it clear that he and many others had not expected Bob to survive that operation and yet he had done so miraculously! He said, "Miraculously!" We thanked him for his efforts and he repeated how it was inexplicable how Bob had made it through this emergency ordeal. We knew though. God's work. Prayer is effective.

Immediately we went to the large window by Bob's bed. There indeed we saw him awake, and, while a bit tired, apparently doing okay, even smiling! We thanked God for His answer to all our prayers. For the first time in a week, I slept soundly all night.

During the course of the next two days Bob had many family visitors, even his sister, Betty, from Knoxville. Bob himself told us that many happy medical people had stopped in to see him, every single one telling him he was a "miracle man," had not been expected to live. We rejoiced for Bob. However, miraculous Bob's survival was, how thankful we all were, we were still not prepared for the glory of hearing God's further confirmation of this miracle. We were not ready for what Bob would tell us his third post-op morning.

When we arrived and "masked up," my son and I found Bob sitting up, apparently in little discomfort. For some reason, he was particularly eager to assure us he was not on any pain medication. He was obviously impatient with our first small chit-chat on arrival.

"Sit down," he urged us from his bed. "And listen!"

I remember being struck by the look on Bob's face. It was a mix of serious and glad. There seemed to be a look of enjoyment that he was about to tell us something very special, maybe even a secret! He was certainly anticipating his remarks to us with pleasure.

Bob told us that during the previous night two nurses had come in and read the Bible to him.

At once, I started to interrupt him, to say that, if he'd describe the nurses, I'd be sure to thank them for him. My interruption made Bob impatient. With a gesture, he motioned me to listen, meanwhile with me still way off-task stubbornly thinking how nice of those nurses to do such a thing, taking the trouble of autoclaving the Bible and all.

"No, Rosemary. Just listen!" Bob sternly refocused my attention on his words.

"The first nurse wore a white uniform," he said. "Her nursing cap had a black band on it. She read to me from a black bound Bible. At first I couldn't remember what part of the Bible it was—but now I do. She read to me Matthew 9:20-25 from a black bound Bible. This is where a woman with a twelve-year issue of blood is healed after touching the hem of Jesus' garment. It's imbedded in the same passage, Matthew 9:18, which is the story of the ruler's daughter raised from the dead by Jesus."

"Then the nurse smiled," Bob said, with his own smile.

"You are a miracle as you were not supposed to have lived," she said."

I was speechless! Imagine that! Me speechless! I started to get up to go find the nurse.

Bob told me firmly to sit down and went on, his next words to us, beginning with a fairly cheerful chuckle. It was as if he were gleeful at what he would say next. He beckoned Robert and me a little closer, although he spoke loudly enough.

I remember wondering if he were on pain medication, observing his rather euphoric behavior. Later I learned, to both the doctors' surprise and mine, that he was not using his self-administered morphine.

My reference librarian (My "It's-not-true-if- I-can't-find-it-written-in-a-credible-source-somewhere") husband, the one who wrote intricate astronomy articles and so disliked sci-fi and fantasy, described the second nurse. All along he was watching our faces very closely, as he said,

"The second nurse was *shimmering*! She read the same verses from Matthew from a gold Bible and said the same thing about me being a miracle."

Bob repeated the whole story, his face glowing, so happy to have told us all this, and making sure we understood that he had not been sedated or seeing things. We were amazed!

At Moffitt no nurses wear the old days white uniforms or caps with black bands, only scrubs and pastel jackets. Shimmering nurses at Moffitt? Never. Bob had been visited by two angel messengers who confirmed answered prayer. He believed it. We did too. Through Bob, we too heard their message! We thanked God for the gift of healing AND the answer to many prayers. There was my warming realization about that prayer back in my bedroom and my reaching out to touch Him as had the woman in Matthew. Bob had never known I did that. Only God could have known it!

I believed that Bob's experience was somehow to reach and teach me—if I too were listening.

Bob had been given more time and he knew it. We made the most of it—long talks with our sons, family, friends, me. On December 28th, our twenty-eighth wedding anniversary, we renewed our marriage vows with both our sons present. We reviewed scrapbooks and diaries from 1963 on. We laughed and cried. We so prayed and hoped Bob would fully recover, if it were God's will.

However, after almost two grateful God-given months, the melanoma returned with a vengeance. Bob was retreated with a different course of chemicals, but I was told during the process, that in about a month he would die. Later that day, when Bob would again need that assistance with oxygen to survive the chemo treatment, since I was told no other treatment options were available, when that time came, after much prayer, after talking with each son, I made the decision to let Bob slip away. No suffering for my Bob. Even knowing Bob would be safe at home in heaven, it was the hardest thing I've ever had to do.

I will never forget Bob's unusually strong command to me, his glib, stubborn-ear wife.

"Rosemary. Listen!"

Oh, Bob. How I'm trying.

I am to this day still struggling with my stubborn ear and then the "do" what I'm told. I'm getting better at this wonderful experience, but not always successful. I still think of Bob's never telling us things unless they were supported by fact. And it comes to me, his story, his definite reprieve from death, is in keeping with his life-long insistence on authenticity. His survival was foretold in the joyful healing and telling of it of Psalm 116 and then confirmed in response to faith and prayer, in Matthew 9:20-25, the Bible, after all, the most credible reference source in the universe, AND all of this confirmed by angels! Wow!

Telling this story to people many times in the past twenty years is apparently not enough for God's purpose. It is with a true nudge that I finally stopped talking and now write about it. I did so first in long-hand, on school notebook paper, in my mountain log cabin. I was rained in for 24 hours. Rather, maybe I was reined in. I'd forgotten my laptop, but never ever this first "be still and hear" awareness story.

# Second Chance Cabin

New widows are often told two things not to do. Quit their jobs or sell their homes and move. We're told we need some time to settle back down, not to do anything too extreme for a while. Well, I didn't sell my home nor quit teaching, though I had startled everyone by almost immediately running off to Russia with colleagues and traveling across Ukraine on an educator's Peace Train! By mid-summer, though, returned from abroad, it was now a mission to East Tennessee up to Ice Water Springs to keep a promise. Bob had wanted his ashes scattered there.

Now back when my Bob and I were in our twenties, it still was a physical challenge the night—yes, night, he and I climbed our way up there to Ice Water Springs as chaperones for a group of hiking teenagers from a church in Gatlinburg. For me it was a very strenuous, long night followed by breakfast at gorgeous dawn in a high perch, chilled, tired, and accomplished.

What would it be like hiking up there now, no longer postponed by travel, still consoled by family and friends, taking my Tennessee Bob home thirty years later, me and my legs much older? As it turned out this time, it would be even a larger challenge for me. Yet, I thought I'd walked my feet off back in Florida on some of our more rolling roads in preparation. Fortunately, I was accompanied by my sons, experienced Eagle Scout hikers, who back-packed their Dad's cremains and a small tree to plant as a memorial. Also with us were Bob's long-time friend, Sugg Carter, a wise mountain man; Bob's sister, Betty; her grown son, John 3; and my tri-athlete sister, Libby. My elderly parents drove to Tennessee with us, but opted to stay below in a Gatlinburg motel until we returned from the mountain.

I'd prayed for strength and not to get too emotional, although it had only been a few months since Bob's death. We set out from mountainside-parking lot and, after only a half mile of fairly even terrain, we hit serious grade. At once this hiking mission became an intense chore for me, one that I couldn't quit. With God's help, though, I did manage to reach Ice Water Springs. What we saw there was most disheartening, There was litter everywhere. I hated the thought of this spot being Bob's final resting place. Sugg decided for us that this was not the place. We should have Bob's service about two miles farther up—walking up a then dry, but uneven creek bed to Charlie's Bunion—a huge outcropping with a spectacular view.

We followed Sugg as guide, although later he would say that we probably shouldn't have hiked those extra two miles, as I was exhausted and so sad. Hike we did, though, finally reaching a spot in the narrow path where we could all sit, remember Bob, pray, and scatter his ashes.

Just as we were about this memorial moment, pink mists suddenly rose from both sides of the towering, raggy rock. I just could not finish the task.

My boys did it for me. Then I felt agonizing loss, the hug of my nephew, and, strangely, relief. In a stupor, I was guided down by family and friends, my nephew, the boys, Sugg, taking turns talking to me, walking beside me as in a foggy dream.

My boots were too big. I stumbled over my own feet and smashed myself on a rock, bloodying my face and leg. Still, I managed, with all their help, to get back down that mountainside in the gathering dusk and light rain, limping to a warm shower and bed. Starving, I could eat nothing.

There was something, though, I told my sister, so final, and yet, something, in all that awful moment, which gave me great comfort, maybe something to come. I hoped she and my parents could not hear me shrieking in the shower. My prayer, as I fell into that deep sleep, aching in so many ways, was that, when I awoke, there would be some respite from the deep loss I now really felt.

My sister later told me that they'd all heard my wails. She also noted that there were paintings of Tennessee on our motel walls, above my particular bed, one of Charlie's Bunion. I saw nothing.

Two days later, by now me with a black eye and still sore, the boys, the twins actually then 24, and I camped out on the banks of the French Broad River over in Del Rio, Tennessee, near Newport. Sugg Carter had introduced us there to his friends, the McCumbers, who owned land on the riverfront and we'd been invited to pitch tents there. Everyone thought it would be good for me to have some outdoor fun with the boys before they had to leave for their California homes.

Come suppertime, we'd decided to make a campfire pot of chicken stew, so took ourselves down to Food City to pick up the ingredients. None of us suspected that a simple trip to the grocery store would be the beginning of two decades of God's plans to comfort me and use me, much less the start-up of a remarkable grief project!

As we were leaving the store, Kenyon, the civil engineer son, spotted an ad in a throwaway paper. It was for the Doak Lamb cabin, back over in Del Rio. "Yours for only $5,995.00," it read, "IF you will just move it away!"

I remember wondering about that IF. How much would it cost if I did this? How complicated could this be if so? If Rosemary just has a cabin in the mountains. We've always wanted one. Right? Hey! This was not quitting my job or selling my house, was it? It seemed such a simple idea. As I look back, it's a really good thing that I didn't analyze the whole thing too closely. How could I take on such a task, such expense—from seven-hundred fifty miles away where, notice, I was still teaching? Naw. Not a good idea IF I'd thought it through.

Instead? "Wonderful!" I thought. I'll buy a little of the mountain beauty we'd all loved and camped in together. I'll enjoy the peace of it when I can, when not teaching school in Florida."

I, Rosemary, had decided.

Just how realistic is that? Other folks have been doing it for years. I actually made myself think it sounded simple enough. However, hadn't I asked God to comfort me? So maybe this was the answer—comfort, just for Rosemary. I could do this. Notice the emphasis on I. I certainly was thinking about myself and taking a whole lot for granted. Didn't really talk to God much about it—a simple asking for help in my grief was all, nothing about should I take on an 1830's log home!

Went ahead. Actually it was intriguing to me that nobody tried to talk me out of it. You would have thought this project would have ranked right up there with the idea about not quitting your job or selling your house. Bought six acres of land, three lots blanketing the lower reaches of a mountainside—bought it from the McCumbers or rather from them as guardians for their physically-challenged son, David, who lived just down the road. Of course, I went and bought the log house—really not a cabin—to put on the land.

We had the old place disassembled, a real feat, the materials carried across the river by flatbed truck to the new site. No problem—so far. Blissfully, and acting as a modern, prideful, resourceful, pioneer widow woman, I never realized then, that I had also bought and carried along many difficult items. None the least of these were my conviction of my own independence and my poor listening habits, that is, where God was concerned. If I'd been paying closer attention then to God's direction, any attention at all, I might likely have actually enjoyed the huge task of rebuilding that cabin which followed. Instead, I found it a persistent, very resistant almost nightmare.

First, the land parcel first purchased needed special drainage and shoring up because of the way the site was cleared. Next, a second adjacent lot, where the cabin was to sit, required build-up, hard to believe, 200 truckloads of soil from elsewhere! My sons had to put in a foundation with piers down sixty feet to rock! There came even more unexpected delays—extremely cold weather, extended rains, a flood that cut us off from the property, and contracting delays. I began to think the logs, although covered, were going to rot away! I learned later, that many of my growing number of local church and community friends thought the same thing! Maybe "strong widow woman" wasn't all that able to do it by herself after all? Still I kept hoping that we would soon start rebuilding what I now called the house, Rose Hill Cabin!

In the meantime, I was teaching and running up and down 1-75 and across I-40 between Florida and Tennessee, often during school breaks. A year was going by already. While waiting the start of rebuilding, I began to write a book, a history of the cabin, interviewing many of the older folks who were associated with the place. I began attending, as an associate member, little Mulberry Gap United Methodist Church way up Highway 107, the other end of the valley from the house site. The Rose Hill project, in its long wait, was actually helping me build a new and different life and an association with Tennessee quite different from that of my student days over at Maryville College and at Knoxville's University of Tennessee. I found I was grieving less as I focused more on this thorny Rose Hill Cabin thing.

Although it was wonderful in this mountain community, when would my Rose Hill Cabin dream come true, though? MY dream would come true, wouldn't it?

Just as I thought the reconstruction would finally get underway, trees and land ready, weather reasonable, I had to look for a new contractor. The first one, who had taken the house down, labeled every single log, who had created a rebuilding grid, suddenly decided he wanted additional money—another $10,000, much more money than he had originally contracted with me to do this rebuilding job! He was adamant. I knew I just couldn't do it. I couldn't and wouldn't! We went our ways. Now just about everybody began to worry I was really going to lose the old logs waiting in the field down below the site.

I searched for another contractor in earnest. Notice it was I alone again doing the main agonizing and the searching for MY project. Big I. Big MY. Concerned local friends were also out hunting log-home builders too. Over the next year and a half, many skilled and experienced men came along to look at the logs, to jawbone about the project, and estimate the cost. However, the estimates were always either outlandishly high or so frighteningly vague, I would not have dared take the chance. The time-lines for start-up and completion were even more outrageous or indefinite. Some people probably didn't really want the daunting task, so they said they were "covered," or it would be months before they could take on the Rose Hill project. By then, I began to think, the logs would truly become dead wood, fit only for a huge and expensive bonfire!

Would I ever find someone to save Rose Hill? Was there someone who could catch the vision I had caught? A key to the answer came when a friend of mine from Florida, a builder, heard my story and decided that he would " do" the house. Was this at last the answer? However, while he did put in the sub-floor, build a picnic table and sawhorses, he quickly discovered that he was unable to find a work crew in town. He couldn't imagine it! Was everyone employed or just lazy? Neither. He decided it was because he was an outsider.

Whatever the reason, this new blind alley, his running up against a so-called log wall, made him furious, made me despair. Maybe I wasn't supposed to be having a log house in the mountains, a retreat just for me. I thought maybe God didn't want me to have this place after all. However, even while thinking this, did I ask God's specific help or listen for guidance in the matter? Not really.

Then in a moment, there was a crack in my stubbornness. So caught up was I with my pitiful "oh-so-sad-why-couldn't-I-have-my-way-with-this-project thinking," that it took a dramatic incident to wake me to the real reason why the Rose Hill project was stalled. In his frustration at his inability to build Rose Hill, my friend, the one who had actually had me buy a sturdy motor puller to lift and place the lower floor logs, started telling me to walk away from the whole project! Even though he knew my dream, he was saying I should quit, cut my losses, give up!

"Just leave it," he said. 'It's not going to happen."

When in tears I told him I just couldn't drop this dream, it meant too much to me, he suddenly said,

"You trust God, more than you trust me."

I was sitting on the steps he had fashioned, there among the sunny trees at the someday front door. In that moment, I began to realize what the real difficulty was with the Rose Hill Cabin project—me! I was trying to do it all by trusting in myself—fancy that—without really seeking God's help! No wonder the time was slipping by and the logs starting to rot, the project going nowhere!

I turned and told my friend." Yes. That's right. I do." But I knew that I really hadn't yet trusted God enough—not about Rose Hill.

The very next day, I was down on the road below the house site with Billy Lamb, the man from whom I'd bought the cabin. Now good friend, with his tractor he was over reorganizing the log pile for a third time, making sure the logs were securely covered. He had an eye out for snakes in the pile. I found myself telling Billy that I was now asking God to help me. How obvious now. How sluggish I had been, how stubbornly independent, ineffective. No wonder Rose Hill was not yet built. It was God's house, not mine, and, if He wanted it built, I must ask only Him to send me the builders. It had been two years. Despairing, that morning I finally gave up Rose Hill to God and gave in to God's wishes for it—if any.

Later that same day I had a call where I was staying from Larry McCumber. I was to call one John Thacker of T & L Builders right there in the same Cocke County, in the Cosby community—an experienced log home builder. He wanted to build Rose Hill! He wanted to do it right away and for the balance of the money that I had promised to the first builder! Saved! Rose Hill would be saved! John Thacker and crew clearly, joyously, obviously, were an immediate answer to my prayers! Answer to a stubborn woman's prayers, one who thought she could do it all by herself—who did not stop to pray about it and then listen.

John brought over his two sons and a friend. All were Christians. They began clambering over the logs. After they'd heard my story of the prior difficulties surrounding Rose Hill, we all agreed in awe that these men's coming was a true answer to prayer. We prayed together at the start of the project for safety and success. I'd learned that Rose Hill Cabin was God's house, not just mine. I now prayed that, as time went by, I would find out more about His purpose for it. Meanwhile, my stubborn heart and ear had learned one more glorious lesson about asking, listening, and doing. My grieving was now solidly replaced with assurance and gratitude and happy hope.

Through screamingly cold weather John and crew would gradually rescue all the large logs, floor joists and hand-stripped pole beams with their original wooden pegs, carefully putting them back in place, until, still not yet chinked Rose Hill Cabin—log home from the 1830's— stood tall once again!

I came up once from Florida and sat up on the hill above the house site, looking down at these worker bees, watching floor on cabin floor growing toward me. Often, during hot soup and sandwich breaks, I sat with them on logs. We talked about God, His work, and workers. We knew then so well that Rose Hill Cabin was coming back—for a special reason.

My research and writing the Rose Hill Cabin book also was finishing, just as the cabin began a new phase of its history, getting its second chance. As the log structure finally neared completion, I asked John Thacker a question. I wanted to know why he actually took on my terribly precarious project which was nearing disaster and certainly not a potentially high-stakes financial plum. After all, his "real work" is designing and building beautiful, brand new, hand- hewn log homes. Had he been told by God to come over and do it?

John smiled that friendly smile of his and quickly gave me his five reasons.

First, he didn't like to see someone alone like me struggling so hard. Then, two, he wanted to have his company known in these parts as a dependable, hardworking builder who does it right, providing good workmanship. Thirdly, he wanted the challenge of putting this giant jigsaw puzzle back together, to see if he could.

Fourthly, there was an historical reason. We don't use the same building techniques as back then, so we should not lose track of our American heritage craftsmanship which brought us to where we are today."

I liked his last reason best:

"I have a vision of what this place was and a dream of what it can be, the weather and Godwillin'."

"God-willing, especially," I thought. He not only was willing for the cabin to finally reappear, but was mightily able in His own special plan for it, sending a Christian building team over to manhandle His logs! God began for me, on that day, a Christian adventure that to this day is still unfolding. For what purpose then, Rose Hill? I'd find out later as both my prayers and my stubborn ear's listening improved, in God's time. Meanwhile. I was trying to listen better, then, obey.

# East on a Russian Peace Train

Even for me, my good friend and colleague, Carole Popaden, thought it very odd that on the very day in February, 1992, that Bob died, I mentioned to her that I was thinking of going to Russia in June, to an educators conference! Would she care to come along? My other colleague, John Hancock, also thought it bizarre when I talked to him about heading for Moscow during the reception for Bob's memorial church service. However, these kind friends said nothing at those first moments about my surprising timing. As it turned out, each would accompany me on that life-changing Russian journey the day before school was out for that summer.

To say that we were drawn to visit Moscow and take a Peace Train across Ukraine and back is actually an understatement. From the moment the three of us spoke of the opportunity, we were going. After all we had been online with a sister school #141 in Moscow for a year and had even interviewed Russian teachers who had participated in the barricaded standoff against the former Soviet Union government, not unlike the Americans at Concord and Lexington. Even then I felt somehow I was supposed to be going. Yet it didn't cross my mind it was the Holy Spirit's nudging toward some special plan.

Before I left Clearwater I made a proposal to the *St. Petersburg Times*. Bob Henderson, the paper's philanthropic community-minded columnist for years, made an agreement with me that I would write and fax back three articles on our trio's unique sojourn for the publication. It was before we had electronic personal transmission. Faxing back from the former Soviet Union was a feat, a story for another book, accomplished mostly through very time-consuming stops at post offices along the way.

And so we were off to Moscow. We did not know where we'd be staying—oh, yes, with homestays, but who knew exactly who these hosts were until we arrived, were assigned, and had walked up five flights of stairs to our digs? Carole and John and I were in different flats and in each there was little or no English spoken. And for the first time in my memory, nobody at home could have reached me, if they'd wanted to—at least for that one night, a scary idea.

Famed Moscow—very hot in summer, no AC, and no screens on the windows! We learned much about having to make do and much about hospitality. We met teachers and students from our sister school and we heard wonderful Russian music. In short, it was an exotic dream, a naive time to go there, just after first freedom began and before all the later economic turmoil, factions vying for control, and the struggles to understand living capitalism. I began to fax back to the *Times* information on pirogies, ballet, youth palaces, and war memorials.

Soon the educational conference was over. I believe the Holy Spirit really took my hand, as I was tired. I was tired from the emotional loss and responsibilities of the previous spring, tired of being fully immersed in another culture and its language, however friendly the hosts, tired from what seemed interminable walking to most places, walking miles to everywhere. 1 was very unused to long walking. Our Russian folks were very accustomed. Yet it was obviously painful for them to see us pay even a few dollars for a cab, when those few dollars were to them a month's wages. So we stopped trying to take cabs. Few of the teacher hosts had a car. After a few days, if the destination was not near a subway station, I adjusted (somewhat) to walking almost everywhere at a very demanding clip.

Really weary, one midnight I struggled aboard the Peace Train '92 headed by Dr. Zoya V. Zarubina, famed for decades as a fighter for peace. For ten days Dr. Zoya would be hosting over a hundred and fifty educators from 12 countries on a comfortable, modern private train. The train had nine cars, each with 10 sleeping compartments. I would share an air-conditioned compartment with Carole. John was way up front in with another American male teacher, but lacking A/C. Each compartment had two beds that served as couches by day, with cubbyholes for clothes and supplies, a table for eating and writing between the beds. We would discover that the compartments would be far more, our little homes away from home, places for wide-open door visiting, yet quiet spots when we could seek a respite from the taxing, constant off-train visits to darling rosy-cheeked dancing children in schools and intensely silencing war memorial fields and massive monuments.

Aboard the train it was not unusual to talk about Bibles, of which there were few in Russia then and the next moment of talk, as if of equal importance, to be queried about what cars we owned. We were frequently asked for the hour of our birth and birthdates as many on the train believed in numerology and were very superstitious. For example, it is considered bad luck to give someone flowers in an even number. Three roses are fine. I found these ideas spooky, not quaint, and unacceptable in those people who also professed to be Christian.

My nightly prayers were notably for my far-away loved ones and for strength to complete our journey. I petitioned that those of us, really few in the train assemblage, Christians, would be an example to those who were not. Yet, it never occurred to me to listen for any special directions in God's plans as we went about our travels. It also never occurred to me there was any particular danger in traveling about this way, even when we were detoured from visiting the republic of Moldava because of civil strife there. Thus, after Moscow, our first memorable stop was Zaporozhye, Ukraine. Zaporozhye would be remembered for many reasons.

Looking back, it is clear that my visit to Zaporozhye was actually God's whole reason I was off to Russia in the first place. At home I had asked Him for some peace from my grief and for strength to move on. Those prayer answers were coming to me even when I first approached my colleagues about the trip. But I didn't really listen and realize these were answers. Seemed more like a diversion or challenge or both, which was exactly the point. The answered prayer involved diversion and challenge.

As it was, the rail detour did serve God's purpose. From the moment we pulled in to the World War Two vintage train station at Zaporozhye, the kind with steps up to the station, a walkway through the little terminal, and then steps down to the street on the other side, amid a tumultuous welcoming crowd, all the planned events to the very moment I write these words twenty years later, there was something singular about the visit. Just the crowds with singing children and people so happy to see Americans (about 25 of our group were Americans) and a peace train arrive. Then, I only knew that we'd reached Zaporozhye, Ukraine, for a three-day layover. I'd never heard of the place. Neither had Carole or John, and he teaches geography. We only knew we were thousands of miles from home and that it was ferociously hot!

Turned out that Zaporozhye, located on the Dniepper River, was, for years, a high security spot in which high-tech aviation materials were manufactured, a city where foreigners, much-less Americans, were not permitted. We were the first group of Americans to visit the city in the last 75 years! The freedom mode was so new in July, 1992, that we were actually asked not to take pictures even of ourselves on the street by several strange men clad in heavy, dark overcoats despite the tortuous weather! Yet, at every turn, ordinary people would hear our English gibblegabble as we walked along and plead with us to come back with them to their homes just so they could talk with us about America. Some even asked if we knew their relatives in New Jersey or New York!

It was in this scene of happy and welcoming confusion that I went back to the train and finished packing my overnight backpack. Crossing the track again, I took myself back up the steps to the platform and out the door to the streetside steps, hurrying to catch up with our train crowd gradually boarding a waiting bus. I was one of the very last persons off the train. Just as I started to descend the steps on the outside, a young, but matronly appearing woman suddenly took my arm and asked in very clear English,

"Are you troubled?"

I was so startled to be asked such a question, for a moment I had to think whether I really was having a problem. I did notice that standing beside her was an older man with a long beard. He was dressed in a long black cossack, that I surmised rightly was clerical garb.

"Why no," I responded, still surprised.

"Why do you ask?"

Here's where God began to get my attention, but still I was not really listening!

"We noticed you have a Bible sticking out the back pocket of your backpack."

She was referring to that small Bible Bob had given me that I always carried with me. It still was covered with the lacey material it sported when I carried it in our wedding more than twenty-eight years earlier. It was indeed peeping out of the top of my backpack pocket—but it couldn't possibly be seen there clearly as a Bible. But to Natalya and her companion, Bible it was.

Before I could figure out why they thought my Bible in view meant I had a problem, she introduced herself very formally,

"I am Natalya. This is Father Feddey," saying this, as she pointed to the minister. "I am his translator and he wants to talk with you about something very important."

As all this was said, we were descending the steep street-side stairs sort of sideways, my mind on rejoining my group, I was thinking that a matter of importance must mean they thought I was Dr. Zoya to whom I quickly referred them. But, no, Natalya and Father Feddey insisted that they wanted to talk with me, even though I was, as I knew very well, not an important person on the train. About what matter of importance could these two wish to talk with me?

Mind you, notice that I was really not listening to what God had in mind at all. It could not have much more plain, so many clues were there right in my face, if I had been paying attention. Take that these folks picked me out because of my Bible and there was a minister seriously trying to talk with me as I stepped off a train from my home thousands of miles away. A teenager would probably reply, "Duh! "if allowed. It should have been so very obvious to my stubborn ear.

Natalya quickly explained that Father Feddey, a Russian Othodox minister, had just been asked to found the first-ever Religion and Bible Studies Department at Zaporozhye University. What a challenge it was to be in a country that had long been officially atheist, she related. The minister was already caring for a very sick wife and the daily operations of both an orphanage and an elder care facility!

She went on breathlessly as they picked up speed with me, all of us descending crab-like toward the now nearly-filled, not to be missed, Peace Train buses and cars now taking my fellow passengers off to who knew where to lodge.

"What he really wants is to see if you can get us some help for the orphanage and for one little crippled boy."

By now I was hearing, but still not a God's girl, listening. I was astounded! Of the whole train these people were clearly singling me out as the one who could help them. They'd probably already been talking to the others ahead of me, but now they had fixed on me. Nothing I could say, no doubts that I had about being able to do anything, seemed to deter the two of them. Finally, I took my leave of them as I popped on a small van waiting to transport us and plopped down beside Carole.

Why was I sighing with relief? Didn't it make any difference to me that I had just heard a very reasonable and desperate plea on the street? Would I have talked with these same people asking these same things back home on the street? Boy, even hearing all that, was I ever stubborn!

The rest of that day was high adventure. Carole and I and a few others were taken to an island where an old estate had apparently been converted into a hotel. We were given spacious second floor rooms, shown where the shower-rooms were, notice I said shower-rooms, not bathrooms, and told how to go down to the river spa and to the cafeteria. We did manage to eat a delicious lunch and then Carole and I started looking for a restroom. We did not find one near the dining room nor up in the shower rooms. We finally asked downstairs and were given a guide to locate the facility, or so we thought. Moments later the guide took us outdoors and walked with us down a hill, where we by then expected to find a detached bathroom of some type. I noted the guide was carrying bathroom tissue. We continued down a long path, yet we could not spot any outbuilding, any building at all!

Suddenly, we realized the situation! We were expected to relieve ourselves out in the open woods. We begged off and returned quickly to the main building in a quandary about what to do. Just then we were told to go get our things, this because we were in the wrong place. Waiting for us was a military vehicle with stern, armed guards. We were motioned into the jeep and careened away without a further word during the trip, away from our so-called lodging to rejoin our group at another hostel where we had been missed and where there were inside toilets. It was an experience to write home about.

The next day, once again here came Father Feddey and Nataly, animatedly joining up with our group. While they did speak to others, during the course of all the three days, they would often reappear at my side from time to time, even joining me at a table on a three-hour boat tour the Peace Train folk were taking on the river. Each time their requests were the same. Still I repeatedly voiced my doubts to them about what I could do. I actually asked that they talk with the others about this. I was not very convincing apparently.

Of course, as I see it now, I was still not listening to God. I stubbornly kept refusing to accept any responsibility for obtaining help for this minister. After all, how could I do so, so far from this city? I didn't want to promise and then let them down! Note, not only was I not listening to God, I was also failing to recognize the matter of these special needs was already in His all-powerful hands. He would proceed to show me what He could and would do even, with my whiney attitude and dragging feet. What was I thinking of?

If any of the days in Zaporozhye, a place not sure yet it was free, was honestly any hotter than any another, our third day there was the worst, even for us Floridians. We were back at the train station preparing to leave. We were actually standing on the tracks and practically desperate about being very thirsty, extremely eager to board our cooler train, at its first call to do so.

Unfortunately, our water purification device was on the train. We begged John and some other of his American train cronies to go back into town and get us SOMETHING to drink. They were good finders. They soon returned, arms loaded with bottles of Fanta Orange and Pepsi Cola. The bottles cost a dime each and were the smallest bottled sodas we had ever seen. The familiar beverages in them were not lukewarm, nor even tepid. They had been sitting in the sun in a storefront and were very nearly boiling! Never mind, we each drank a bottle in one swig and, to our minds, considered it the best taste from our distant home ever!

Immediately after our Pepsi-Fanta party, Natalya reappeared, this time without Father Feddey. She said he had a university meeting, but he had wanted to wish us good-bye. She was now doggedly determined to get me to accept their joint pleas. By this time the special needs requests were packaged in a blue pasteboard folder that gave off a very sour gluey smell. Inside the bulging packet, I learned later, were many proposals, all typed on very yellowed paper. Some of the pages proposed setting up business connections. However, most sheets addressed the needs of the children and elderly people under Father Feddey's care. One fragile sheet concerned a crippled boy named Artyem. His super-serious little picture was enclosed matter-of-factly with everything else and the lot strapped around with a white cotton strip of string.

As Natalya stood there with me literally in the tracks, our group started boarding the train for our next stop at Kiev. Once again she pressed the packet into my hands, pleading I take it and do something. Her insistence finally won my grasp. Very reluctantly, I took the packet and said good-bye, deep concern about what I'd done probably showing on my face and relief definitely showing on hers. Minutes later, as our train slowly moved out of the station, I watched Natalya back there on the tracks watching us. With a final wave she turned, and, mission accomplished, threaded her way back across the tracks in high heels with no hose, not an uncommon habit for women we met over there.

And so Zaporozhye was behind us. In front of me in my lap lay a folder filled with things God wanted me to listen about and act on. Listening I'd certainly not done well. And I still wasn't paying close attention to what I was supposed to be doing for God.

While there were many other adventures along our way before we reached the United States and our homes. I'll not share much detail, as Natalya's pathetic blue packet is the real focus of this awareness episode.

We did visit Kiev, there, I faxing home to the *Times* a long train story about Zaporothye, with some details about the orphans and elderly gleaned from the smelly blue packet, those details only just barely sandwiched in with the river boat trip, the pitiful and dying Chernobyl children we'd heard performing a haunting operetta, the impressive schools and memorials in Belarus, and the world-class museums in St. Petersburg (formerly Leningrad).

Home! So full of our adventures were we, it was a month before we began to spin out the grand tales of all that happened toward our friends and relatives. Actually, I realize now I was full of myself. However, on my voice mail, the very day I returned, there was a message that at once taught me a higher awareness about the workings of the Holy Spirit through believers, like me, even when we're not listening. As my mother would have put it,

"It brought me up with a round turn."

The message was from Harvest Temple Church on Walsingham Road right here in my county! Members had read my article published in the *Times* long before my arrival. Just imagine my surprise when I learned that in three days a team would be leaving on a mission trip to Zaporozhye, Ukraine! Would I please contact them with details of the things most needed which they might take with them to Father Feddey's charges!

There was really nothing mysterious at all about my being part of God's plan to answer the desperate prayers and pleas from His ministering Ukrainian who was so worried about the children and aged that he approached touring Americans who accidentally detoured his way off their train for a little stay! I had not listened while in Ukraine, only now I began to see the clear call for my help as part of God's grand design—note, of which I could see I was playing a part. Notice He let me see this glimpse when I listened to my voice mail!

I spent the next three days getting money and goods from friends and family and helping the mission bound Harvest Temple group pack for their trip. We sent several large cartons with warm baby clothes, pediatric aspirin and cough syrup, juvenile thermometers, band-aids, as well as similar medicines geared for senior citizens, products that Father Feddey could not have obtained in 1992, even if he had had the funds. Maybe not even now.

According to the returning Harvest Temple members, Father Feddey considered the entire episode from Rosemary, the writer on train sending word home, to mission field visitors and needs met, as a glorious answer from God. It would be hard to mistake the timing of it all as anything else but. What a lesson! The Holy Spirit arranged to let me hear then the reports of the American visitors holding sick and forlorn children in their arms and helping dress and feed them. What a lesson also in listening, in awareness of some of God's plans, an antidote to my earlier stubbornness and resolution to do better, genuinely listen and then do!

So at least some help had gone over to Zaporozhye's needy children. What then of the crippled child named Artyem? While in Zaporozhye the Harvest Temple mission group heard about him too, but did not meet him. I began to worry about the boy. He was on my heart. He was seven years old in the photo I had of him, but what could I do? "Why me, anyway?" I kept asking myself. I was thousands and thousands of miles away in this world from that one child. An inner voice told me the answer. At the urging of the Spirit, while I was already awake, I suddenly awoke to the realization no longer of, "Why me?" now, "Of course, me!" Who else on the Peace Train lives only one half hour over the causeway from Shriners' International Headquarters and less than an hour from one of the free Shriners International Hospitals for Crippled Children? God certainly knows the geography of the Earth He created, even if I was foggy on it living right here in it! God is not only All-Present, All-Powerful, and All Knowing. He is the most patient Father waiting on our listening and obedience, using even that slow growth to move along his wonderful plans.

The Ukrainian boy's story of his coming to America is included later in this volume as continuing testimony about the admonition to listen, know, and then do.

# Following Directions

Well, don't we spend our days trying to follow directions, somebody's, if not our own? Seldom though do we follow the specific ones God sends to us. That seemed the case until some of us actually decided to bring that Ukrainian boy to the USA for treatment that was then not available, even denied him, in his own country.

When I said yes, such as did the woman the angel directed to go and tell disciples about Christ's rising in Matthew 28:5-7, I thought it meant simply giving my address as a legal place for Artyem and his father to stay while in the USA while he received treatment for a crippling birth defect arm condition called arthogyposis! Simple? No!

Wow! Here Artyem and his dad came and to no surprise, really. He was supposed to because Shriners Hospital for Children, across the world from him, happened to be just moments from the Tampa airport!

Upshot? In seven weeks, the youngster gained 10 pounds, grew an inch, and could lift those disabled arms out of the swim pool water. Not cured, but he was taught extensive physical and occupational skills. He flew home hopefully for a better life, this because we truly listened to God's plan while on that far-away train and, when back at home, also did as bidden.

Afterward this whole awareness episode with Artyem, led me to write this following devotion for me and others, one entitled, Following Directions. It started with reading Proverbs 3:5-6 and also Matthew 28:5-6 (KJV), models for listening and following directions. In the latter passage, for example, at the open tomb, an angel tells the woman to go quickly and tell the disciples that Christ is risen! She hears this and does as instructed— at once!

The beginning of a sty, a swelling on my eyelid, I thought on waking. Although I had a busy day ahead, I'd have my doctor take a look immediately. Since my regular physician was away, I was assigned a substitute, Dr. Evelyn Moise', who, with her husband, then headed a new teaching hospital at the University of Haiti. I recalled my only trip to Haiti, how I'd been stunned at the nearly hopeless condition of its children. My visit was long before the earthquake, floods, and rampant disease in recent years compounded the already horrific situation.

When Dr. Moise' came in, I immediately found myself asking her, "How can I help with pediatric medical supplies for the clinic?" She closed the door and began to cry— with joy!

"God told me someone would come," she said. "Children there are dying for lack of oxygen therapy. We need pediatric-sized oxygen regulators, inhalators, and nebulizers!"

Within two days my church circle and the mens' missions group provided money for equipment, acquired at discount from a supplier who had been involved with Artyem's visit. Now it was to save sick Haitian children! Later I learned the day of my office visit was the only one on which Dr. Moise' had substituted at that office. Oh, yes. She found nothing wrong with my eyelid. Instead I could clearly see that God had directed me to accomplish a special mission quickly! Not only was this pediatric medical mission a sudden success, the women's church circle involved with it began a now more than decade long mission in this area, both domestic and foreign, continuing God's bidding about pediatric missions to this day.

Here is a prayer I prayed then and now:

Lord, thank You for Your specific, all-knowing nudges, for loving tasks in Your Name, especially to care for children with extreme medical needs. As I am still and listen, I learn that You are truly with us always. Let me hear directions and give me strength to follow them. Amen

# God's Priorities

Even while organizing this book and repeatedly stating that I'm determined to listen to God and His message for me, His directions, still I find myself often being just too busy to seriously concentrate on this listening I'm supposedly trying to do. Like, wasn't that the mail delivery out there just then? Or, guess the neighbor just got home. I'll tell her about the leaking faucet. Or did I call my friend back about going out to supper later?

In this, as frequently the case, I try to take myself by the collar and replant myself, in this case, here at the keyboard or over at a table with my prayer journal notes. Doesn't always work. Then the busy day is over, too bad, the author now too tired will do the writing and listening tomorrow morning, feeling rested, fresh. Yeah, right!

As Jesus by the sea directed brothers Simon, called Peter, and Andrew, fishermen, to leave their nets and follow him to become fishers of men. (Matthew 4:18-22), they heard Him, stopped what they were doing and followed. At once! They listened and did His bidding, His priority. So must I when I really reconsider how my days roll out.

Still, there seems to be increasingly more to do each day than can be done. There's also more frustration at what's left undone, than satisfaction at accomplishment. I keep thinking, I'm just too busy to attend, to plan, to respond, even just to relax. However, too busy to pray, to worship, to LISTEN?

The phrase "too busy" actually means far more than not enough time for me to do some task. I have plenty of time every day. God gives it to each of us. It has to do with priorities. His Great tasks, ours not so great. Definitions for "too" include *excessively* and *to such a* degree *as to be regrettable!* "Busy" means both *engaged in activity* and also *meddling!* Wow, that last definition fits lots of times!

The Bible in Luke 10: 38-42 (KJV) offers realistic living, listening and doing definitions. Luke reports that Jesus admonished Martha. She was complaining to Him that she was busy serving, while her sister Mary was just sitting there, not helping, just listening to Jesus's words. Martha was indeed meddling, being a busybody literally.

Martha wanted Jesus to make her sister get busy. Jesus told Martha that Mary's choice was what was really needed and good—the priority—for her time that moment.

So what happened next? Imagine. There was Jesus right there for the listening. Did Martha hear Him and at once set aside everything else to listen to His precious words?

Behind me right now is another busy day with a to-do list, some items troubling and time-consuming, exactly in like in Martha's day. Pick up some milk, replace a couple batteries, return some library books, some task left undone, say, a call-back to a truck repair shop.

I'm trying to learn to make time in my day, In fact, I did it today, time for prayer-time, time to call on someone widowed who feels lonely, even time to work on this manuscript, rehashing it all. Do you hear me? I heard that these tasks were God's Priorities for me this day.

I pray, Lord, help me to use the time You have given me in prayer and the service You will for me. I'll try to listen and be busy in that direction. I'll really try. Amen

# What Happens Next Might Be Wild and Scary

After the Angel Visitors and the Russian Peace Train, the sty message leading me out to help with that crippled child and dying Haitian children, listening to God lead by being still leads to ever more adventures, some quite surprising, some quite demanding, others so wonderful, they are actually great rewards for listening and doing God's bidding for me in particular!

Here I refer to Isaiah 43:10—reminder that God owns the opportunities and plans for me. Finally, listening to God, along came more directions:

• I was hired away from my regular teaching assignment, guiding children and teachers in reading, four times, yes, four times, this during my grieving for my first husband, Robert. Can you imagine a public School Board permitting this as part of my emotional recovery from the loss of my husband? I still can't. Good thing, because it was so human far-fetched, I could not have dreamed it up. I was to be the American schoolteacher aboard a Ukrainian cruise ship, docked in the USA at St. Petersburg, Florida. The ship needed American language training for its wait and bar staffs, and for its room cleaners. These ship staff folks spoke British English, but could not communicate easily with Americans, with our speedy speaking of the common slang we use every day. The cruise personnel were thus often misunderstood and deemed rude by American passengers. And I was supposed the "fix?" This came about because someone back in Ukraine recalled my visit there, the disabled boy's visit here, and recommended me?

So aboard. I was treated as crew, but had my own cabin. I loved the work. However, could quite soon tell why God had sent me along. The shocks came quickly, the first, during the first of the three month travels, as numerous women casually told me they'd had abortions while on board, in fact, an extra doctor sailed each quarter just for that purpose! I was unable to offer a sensible response to such a horrific notion. I prayed and asked God what He thought I should do. I listened, but received instead, different directions just for me.

I asked some shipboard workers, a few of my language students, if they had a Bible. Not one did, although most said they were Christians, belonging to the Russian Orthodox church at home. Religion once in the conversation, some acquaintances offered me Kachina-like, maybe voodoo-like dolls, and shared other non-Christian ideas, such as wanting to tell fortunes based on horoscope readings, these beliefs showing clearly serious confusion about Christian faith.

• The second cruise, three months later, I took aboard a large box of Bibles, provided by church friends and a Christian in Tennessee, these printed in English. I planned just to hand them out—all sixty copies.

Imagine my surprise when, as I unpacked the Bibles and arranged them on a table to distribute, I looked up and not only saw the cruise staff members with whom I was working, but many members of the ship's engine room crew from way below decks, mostly men in grubby attire, people I had never even seen before and would likely never see again. Many people had appeared suddenly, now in a line snaking all the way down the passageway from the door of the room where I was asked to give out the books.

God still at work, much I say as in the several loaves and fishes parables, as soon the Bibles, my meager supply, were all given away, I was sad that I'd run out, since many crew members were still waiting in line. Yet, those not given a Bible turned away talking, strangely not seeming at all upset by not having received one.

I really should have known better than second-guessing God. A dining room server who did obtain a Bible apparently saw how frustrated I was at not having enough Bibles for everyone. She shortly informed me not to worry as all would be able to share the Bibles, which seemed quite doubtful to me, just as the fish and loaves distribution, did at first, to those on hand. Faith, Rosemary!

She reassured me. It seemed that every person who had received a Bible was, even as we spoke, meticulously taking it apart, dividing it into many, many "books," or parts of books, say a group of 10 Psalms or a single chapter from the Gospels. Each newly arranged piece was given to an individual to read. Every recipient would later return, turn in the piece they'd read, select another one, more than one hundred persons sharing so all could read the Bible!

The hunger that first ship-wide crew displayed involving those Bibles was way beyond what I'd ever done to get at a Bible, having had several of my very own just given me in my lifetime! This was God and loaves and fishes, God and fragments of his Holy Word, as manna.

• The very next month, a friend, who knew about the dividing of the Bibles distribution experience, called to say she had a source of new Bibles printed in Ukrainian. Did I have any folks who could use them? Within two days, I learned there were right then ten students visiting in or near my Florida city, all living, as had Artyem, with homestays—hospitality homes with students their own ages so they could attend high school with them for the month. We obtained a Bible for each of the students. The students' chaperones told us that back at their homes, hardly anybody had a personal Bible. These students now did and in their own language. The friend who called me was listening. I was listening. God had the specific directions for her and me on behalf of the children. We moved on it!

• Grieving for a husband (or wife) is a very difficult process, I found after actually losing my first husband Robert after 28 years and then my second husband, Marvin, after only three years of marriage. After the family and friends and caring which accompanied both losses, surrounded by friends and family, both times it got quiet finally at home, this welcomed and also sad.

It was God's way of helping me when, after five or six weeks, my pastor, Dr. Tom Farmer, Jr., now retired from my St. Paul United Methodist Church, sent me (and seven others) a personal, strong note inviting us to several sessions at the church with a Christian grief counselor. I hesitated at first because I thought this busy teacher woman was doing just fine. To all appearances, that was absolutely true. However, it also was absolutely not.

During the days that followed Bob's death and memorial service, I was having trouble eating, that, is, regularly. I would just grab something and eat it in the kitchen and get on with schoolwork or reading the letters and cards which came each day—thus every afternoon, those pretty cards and beautiful, supportive wishes became part of my routine from which I could not relax or relieve myself.

I listened to my pastor. He was listening to God about helping us. Helping it did! We first of all met others feeling the same loss and odd responses. That alone made me know these grieving moments were quite normal, if not something any of us ever expected or were sharing before now!

What really, really helped even more, as we sat there around a pretty table in our lovely church parlor, was this kind counselor giving us suggestions of options to ease the pain and transition to our new lives without our lost spouse. Here are just a few of those ideas, restated in my own words;

1. As lovely cards and messages arrive nearly every single day, try this as a relieving response. Get a lovely decorative box. Quickly

look over the arriving message, set aside a check or other item, if sent. Then, place the card in the lovely box to be read several weeks later. It is not necessary to respond or send thank-you notes now or at all, but later is fine. You need your time now to be relaxed, not do homework.

2. Break the eating routine, perhaps stop off somewhere and then come home and sit down at the table. Pamper yourself—you know, placemat, napkin, etc. Eat at different hours, perhaps with a friend. If a holiday, change the habitual event in some major way.

3. It is not necessary to retell the story details about the loss, even to someone say, in church who comes up to you after just learning about your loss. It is understandable just to smile and offer thanks for their caring and then move on to your pew.

The list goes on and there are about a dozen suggestions. What does this have to do with my listening? That little list has become a little ministry for me. When ever I hear about a recent loss, mostly widows among friends, kin, relatives, neighbors, mothers of friends, I wait about two weeks, after the first rush of grief arrives and overwhelms, when those people, as I did, need some realistic ideas to help them move on, I send the short list to them in a simple card.

So far I have sent the list to more than 25 people. From many I have heard replies, although none were asked to contact me. Here is one telling response, however. My former teaching colleague is the daughter of a prominent doctor and community leader. At his passing, his wife of more than 60 years received literally hundreds of cards, e-mails, and letters. I read of the doctor's death, his obituary, right after my devotional time one morning and was nudged to call my friend right then and tell her I was nudged.

I learned at once why I was told to call. My friend's mom, I learned from her, had spent every day of those past few weeks writing thank-you notes for all incoming sympathy mail. She anticipated every mail delivery, both expecting and receiving more beautiful reminders of her lost love and then would immediately sit down to read every one AND answer it, even when it took exhausting hours.

When I told my friend about the first suggestion on the list, she said she knew why I'd called. That very morning, her so-saddened mother had said to her,

"I just can't do this (the thank-yous) any more!"

The list I was to send her would help. However, God having me call my friend quickly provided the new widow with immediate, gentle postponement, "permission," to stop for a while, the relief, from constantly rethinking her loss, relief, which she so badly needed right at that moment.

So now I keep a stack of the grief comfort lists on my desk. I can send it out as needed, as called to do so, which could be anytime, with or without the list even handy.

• Take this morning. Our new Senior pastor, Rev. Bob Martin, preached about how we all face "giants" much as David, when confronting Goliath for the Israelites. We all have giants that God can help us overcome. On the way home, I pulled off the road to look at a driveway sale with a huge poppy painting and many women's shoes.

A man with "Tim" embroidered on his work pocket, with his grown older daughter came out to sell things. Tim tearfully related his wife had died of cancer but three weeks earlier, so he was selling her things, moving. The conversation immediately turned to the giant task this widower was attempting so soon after his loss. Here it was again—the moment to share the grief comfort list! I mentioned the list and St. Paul.

Tim asked, "Did you know Dr. Tom Farmer?" He was amazed it was my pastor, Dr. Tom, who'd sent me to Christian grief counseling when my first husband died of cancer. Here came again the first few to-do things on the "list." He said Tom had provided marriage counseling to his late wife and him. I suggested the St. Paul Outreach Ministry come get the stuff he was trying to sell, that he and his daughter take a breather, begin to move on.

He thanked me. We together thanked God, for Pastor Bob's reminding us that God can help us defeat any giant, grief, a huge one right here, the point.

Oh, yes! Was what happened next in those ongoing listening/doing adventures either wild or scary as in the chapter title? No way. The title might better be, What Happens Next is Definitely Surprising and God-given Amazing!

# And To My Listening Ears!

So the listening to God and then guided doing experience continued.

• My sister and I prayed as to whether or not we should allow a feeding tube for our then aging, late father. We were anguishing over the decision as we were told, once placed, this tube would be permanent. Yet we knew how much our beloved Daddy enjoyed the tastes and flavors of food.

The night before we would have to inform the attending physician, I read Psalm 103: 5 (NKJV) "Who satisfies your mouth with good things." There. Maybe "things" means God's truth, merciful "food." No coincidence. We had the answer to comfort Daddy, even though no decision we made would promise to increase his then fragile health and life span.

• On the porch of my TN log home, Rose Hill, there appeared a couple, neighbors from far down the road, neighbors who wanted to walk through and see the historic cabin. I told the wife to go right ahead in and look around, on her own. After about fifteen minutes, she reappeared on the front porch where sat Peter, my dear third husband, whom I'd met at Rose Hill when he came to recreate the two fireplaces and chimney. The neighbor's husband was sitting there too, talking with Peter.

Her words to me were, "Nothing is in there!"

I knew immediately what she meant. I'd heard she believed in ghosts and other supernatural ideas. She'd assumed my very old house was haunted.

She'd believed she would detect ghosts or spirits inside Rose Hill. That misconception gave me my nudge.

I told her that, of course, there were no haunted aspects of this home, regardless of its long history. Disappointed, she'd found nothing supernatural except for my protective Christian testimonial. We had twice blessed this home—it belonged to God.

• Around Christmas about a year ago I vowed to make the celebration of Christ's Birth more meaningfully Christian as to gifts for my family, especially those kin with children. Stores, even Christian bookstores, just did not yield any practical ideas. After prayer, and unnecessary worry about really doing something meaningful for the younger kin, I received by mail the gift-giving support brochure from World Vision!

Hooray! Once again prayers were answered. I was able to send Christmas cards to my families, cards that would be easy to explain to the children. I provided financial support to projects actually helping children in both the United States and abroad. How about live ducks as a gift to Haitian families, birds that provide meat, eggs, and hatch more ducks! In case of another flood in that place, ducks can swim, not drown!

How about water purifying and filtering equipment for a family there, the gift card sent to a nephew's family here that works with plumbing and pools? How about school supplies for school programs in hard-pressed American communities, this card to young teacher kin? Of course, the real items were actually shipped to those in need. My gift recipients received from me colorful and informative report cards.

• Over the last few years the community in which I live, although remaining a lovely Florida place for me to reside, began to have problems with civility, that is, considering politeness in all dealings, even those which involved hard decisions about the use of money or the methods of those elected to manage things.

The negative feelings that arose from continuing uncivil discussions, began to weary me and many neighbors and residents. In prayer I asked how we could solve this very annoying matter, and nothing seemed to help, at least as far as I was concerned. I prayed, hoping for help from God in resolving the issues. Still no resolution.

I was reading my Bible as part of my devotional time when James 1:19 (KJV) gave me the answer, the idea I was directed to do, my little nudged assignment. I printed out small copies of the verse and now use it to remind me and to give to others. I am directed to be: "swift to hear, slow to speak, slow to wrath." So be the solution.

• For several years I have visited First United Methodist Church in Elmhurst, Illinois, where my son Robert and his family are members. Their pastor, Rev. Dr. Norma Lee Kerns Barnhart, has further encouraged my prayerful listening. A prayer part of each Sunday service is called Time of Silence, during which individuals pray silently.

Recently Pastor further discussed this special congregational moment with me. She'd seen an embroidered plaque reading, "Shhh! I'm praying." She'd later enjoyed another in her office reading, "Shhh! I'm listening."

Am I?

I now know that listening to God applies all the time, that direction is unending, if heard. I believe that my gift from Him of writing ability is to be used to share such experience, once I shut up and listen.

I close this current book with a Biblical passage directed to me:

Psalm 45:1 "My heart is indicating a good matter as I speak of the things I made" . . . "about God;" . . . "my tongue is the pen of a ready writer."

"Ready" in (NKJV) also means *skillful*.

In this case, maybe. Maybe not.